Going Dutch

Dick Pappenheim

Going Dutch

An easy guide to Dutch business culture for expatriates

International Books, 1999

ISBN 90 5727 003 x
NUGI 601
tweede druk, 1999

Illustrations: Jenne van Eeghen, New York

Editing: Niala Maharaj
Cover: Marjo Starink, Amsterdam
Cover illustration: Irene Wolfferts, Amsterdam
Cover photo: ANP foto, Amsterdam
Printing: Drukkerij Haasbeek, Alphen a/d Rijn

International Books, A. Numankade 17, 3572 KP Utrecht,
The Netherlands, tel. 31 (0)30-2731840, fax. 31 (0)30 2733614

Contents

Acknowledgements

As the spouse of a Dutch expatriate, my wife experienced the hardships, as well as the pleasures, adapting to new surroundings, new people and new mores. It is not surprising that, once the tables were turned and we were back in Holland, she gave enthusiastic and unfailing encouragement to my efforts at writing this book. Thank you, Anita!

For the corrections to my English, I owe thanks to Ron Wood, who spent many an afternoon on his terrace at the Côte d'Azur going through the text. In addition, I am grateful to Toon Quarles van Ufford Twiss who, through his thorough knowledge of Dutch history, contributed significantly to the Chapter, "The roots of Dutchness".

Alfred Müller's support was also valuable: without him, I would never have got the workings of the works councils right. Special thanks are equally due to Maut and Martien van Eeghen for their contribution to the chapter "Etiquette".

The title "Going Dutch" was suggested by Loren-Paul

Caplin during a stroll through the streets of Maastricht.

And I am, of course, indebted to the staff and students of The Language Institute, "Regina Coeli", who
supported my efforts in many ways.

If You Have Been Warned ...

For those going abroad on holiday trips or for cultural enrichment, travel guides are often considered a must. The "Baedeker" has long been a household word to British travellers intending to climb the Swiss Alps or study Renaissance Art in Italy, while civil servants posted to former European colonies depended on the "old hands" there to perform introductory duties.

To-day, the travelling public has been greatly expanded, and, with the rapid internationalisation of business, a new class of foreigner has been created— the expatriate. Unlike the Mayflower Pilgrims, or the Huguenots who fled to Holland in the 17th century, the members of this class have not chosen to emigrate to find a new "patria", a new motherland, but have been sent abroad by their employers for a limited period of time.

But whereas the tourist finds his needs catered for in every way, the expatriate is confronted with the harsh reality of everyday life in his new surroundings. His wife will discover that, whilst during their first visit everybody, everybody meaning the taxi-driver, hotel-porter and barman spoke English, the grocer and the butcher do not. At the office, the foreign executive may be confronted with secretaries who question his instructions, and workers' councils who oppose his decisions. He will discover that, in order to make things work, he has to take into account local customs and sensibilities.

This book is meant to assist such a person. It tries to avoid any judgement on "right" or "wrong", "good or bad" regarding the habits attributed to the Dutch. As the French say: "un homme averti en vaut deux", *or* "If you have been warned about what may happen, you have twice the chances of succeeding!"

Note: Although "the Netherlands" is the official name, "Holland" (which refers to only a part of the Netherlands) is how the country is known abroad. We will therefore use "Holland" in this book rather than "The Netherlands".

CHAPTER I

The Main Elements of Dutch Culture and Behaviour

A survey was carried out amongst one hundred expatriates who were studying Dutch at the well-known Language Institute, Regina Coeli. The respondents were asked what was the most striking difference between the behaviour of the Dutch and the norms and customs of their own countries. The most frequent comments about the Dutch were:
- very direct, frank
- informal
- little respect for hierarchy and rank
- thrifty, talk a lot about money
- friendly, open, tolerant
- dress is very casual
- pragmatic, no-nonsense
- less polite, less diplomatic
- many meetings, few decisions
- speak their mind, do not evade confrontation
- bureaucratic, everything is planned.

Needless to say, the Dutch habit of repeated "coffee-breaks" at the office did not remain unmentioned.

Each of these elements will be treated in individual chapters of this book, showing how they influence:
- the social environment
- the business environment.

Of course, not all Dutch people will fit the above description. People differ due to differences in age, intellectual background or regional influences. Elderly people will, as a rule, be more conservative than youngsters. Dutch people educated before the "cultural revolution" of 1968 may differ in attitude from those educated in the 1980's. It is also obvious that, as a group, University graduates will behave somewhat differently from farmhands.

REGIONAL DIFFERENCES

In the same way that Paris is different from the rest of France, Amsterdam is not representative of all of Holland. Officially, the country is divided into 12 provinces, but from a cultural point-of-view there are three main regions:
- the North
- the South
- the "Randstad".

The division between the North and the South is marked by the rivers Rhine and Maas and their tributaries, which enter the Netherlands in the South-east and empty into the North Sea.

People from *the South* (mainly Noord-Brabant and Limburg) have a slightly softer pronunciation, are mainly Catholic, and are said to be more epicurean, or, as the Dutch put it, "Burgundian". Thus, the celebration of Carnival is a great happening in 's-Hertogenbosch, Maastricht and Venlo. All residents participate, and normal life comes to a standstill for five days, as specially-composed songs are sung, and huge quantities of beer are consumed to keep throats in shape for singing.

The North, on the other hand, is mainly Protestant, and carries the marks of Calvinism: religious rigidity, soberness and frugality. Here, carnival is practically unknown, and on Sundays many village pubs are closed. The climate is colder than in the south: in winter, frozen lakes and canals make it the home ground for long-distance ice-skating champions, who, once every so many years, compete in a skating marathon of 200 km., called the "eleven-towns race".

To *the West*, the name *Randstad* is commonly given to the great urbanisation which includes Amsterdam, The Hague, Rotterdam, Utrecht, and their surrounding communities. Together, these cities constitute a metropolis of 6 million inhabitants, where past and present exposure to international trade and migration has created a different culture from that in the rest of the country. There is less rigidity, more openness, and more "avant-garde" attitudes. The influx of Huguenots, Spanish and Portuguese Jews and other persecuted groups in the 17th century has also contributed to a broad, liberal attitude of mind. In more recent times, due to a shortage of unskilled labour, a new immigration wave occurred, with the arrival of workers from Spain, Portugal, Morocco and Turkey. Later, a second wave of immigrants brought asylum-seekers from Africa, the Middle-East and Eastern Europe.

The lion is the national symbol of the Netherlands.

Like New-York, *Amsterdam* has become a multicultural society and also a centre of artistic activities. According to statistics, in the year 2015, 45% of Amsterdam's inhabitants will belong to ethnic minorities.

Rotterdam, the no.1 port of Europe, and one of the largest in the world, takes pride in its businesslike attitude, whilst *The Hague*, which houses the Dutch government and also all foreign embassies, is the centre of the "savoir-vivre".

CHAPTER 2

The Roots of "Dutchness"

"Until the 16th century, we knew Holland only as an obscure swamp, an ambiguous region partly land, partly water, a lump of mud in the mist, flooded at regular intervals by the North Sea and inhabited by unfortunate people who were condemned to an endless fight against the wrath of heaven and the fury of the water."
Ramalho Ortigão (Translation by D. Pappenheim).

Thus begins the book "A Holanda", written 100 years ago by the Portuguese writer and journalist, Ramalho Ortigão. As it proceeds, the author develops an admiration for the way these "unfortunate people" had succeeded in becoming a prosperous and well-managed nation, with a delicate balance between wealth and civilisation. But there is no doubt that the elements, and in particular water, have played an important part in shaping Dutch character.

Water as threat

The need to protect the land from flooding, especially in the western part of Holland forced farmers to join forces in the building of dikes. A monitoring organisation was therefore created with the task of controlling the maintenance of these protective walls, and of keeping a permanent watch on the behaviour of the rivers and the sea, warning the farmers in case of imminent flooding.

Contrary to what was happening in the rest of Europe, where all appointments were the exclusive privilege of counts, dukes and other feudal landowners, the inhabitants of the "low countries" participated in the appointment of wardens who controlled the flow of the water. These "water wardens" set up Regional Councils, which were largely free from interference on the part of the nobility, and which could even impose and collect the taxes necessary for the upkeep and maintenance of the dikes.

Of course, this delegation of authority was also in the interest of the landlords. By encouraging farmers to settle in the region and take responsibility for the control of water, their arable land surface grew and became more productive. This increased the taxes they received.

This partial autonomy of the farmers and fishermen resulted in a society based on collective action, which fostered a sense of community, as well as a spirit of freedom. Thus, in a era when absolute authority was unchallenged in most of Europe, the inhabitants of the

Low Countries were already shaping the first institutions of what we now call democracy.

"The aversion of the Dutch for authority therefore has historical roots!"

Water as opportunity

The geographical position of the Low Countries at the estuaries of the great rivers, Rhine, Maas and Scheldt, contributed significantly to the prosperity and wealth of the region. This applies especially to the Northern part, since what used to be called "The Netherlands" included the greater part of Belgium and in particular the territory called "Flanders".

In the Middle Ages, transport by water was the main means of getting heavy products and produce from one place to another, so trading routes were established between the middle of Europe and the ports on the North Sea. Along the rivers, trading posts came into being which soon developing into regional markets and exchange centres.

In the South, Antwerp, on the river Scheldt, had become a major centre of trade and industry in the 15th and 16th century. But when Spanish troops occupied the city in 1585, the "Hollanders" from the North cut off Antwerp's trading activities by blocking the estuary of the river. Antwerp's role was taken over by its main trade rival, Amsterdam.

Transport by land also played a role in developing these trading centres. One of the well-known routes went from Cologne, through Maastricht and Brussels, to the Flemish port of Brugge.

Another source of wealth was the abundance of fish especially herring in the North Sea.

The inhabitants of the Low Countries were thus involved at an early stage in trading and shipping, not only along the rivers but also on the North Sea and later on the Baltic sea. This laid the foundation for the Dutch to become a naval super-power in the 17th century. Not only did they call at most European and North-African ports; their adventurous spirit took them to the East Indies, which resulted in a lucrative trade in spices and other exotic products. Thus, in the 17th Century, the town of Amsterdam, which housed the headquarters of the United East-Indies and West-Indies Trading Companies, became the wealthiest and foremost trading centre of Europe.

It is hardly surprising that, with this historical background, a mercantile tradition has survived until today, creating an image of the Dutch as
  "a nation of traders and merchants".

Calvinism

The strict doctrine of the sixteenth-century Protestant reformer, John Calvin, and the zeal of the preachers who spread his gospel, left a lasting mark on the North of Holland. (Even the Southern provinces, Noord-Brabant and Limburg, which remained Catholic, have been influenced by the Calvinist way of life.)

Calvinism stood for:
- unconditional adherence to the Bible and the holy scriptures in all aspects of life
- strict personal discipline in obedience to the Almighty's teachings
- the State's maintenance as a devout institution, in which all public bodies and authorities were expected to support and protect the (authentic) Calvinist Church
- an abhorrence of the temptation of sin, the greatest danger to the human soul, whose only chance of redemption was through sober and frugal living.

Obviously, this precept of frugality was at odds with Holland's great prosperity in the 17th and 18th centuries, and constituted a serious moral dilemma for wealthy Dutch traders and bankers. The book "The Embarrassment of Riches" by the historian *Simon Schama* gives a vivid and detailed picture of how these moral problems and constraints were dealt with.

In to-day's culture, the following elements of Calvinist teaching can still be noticed:
- a tendency to frown upon spending money on luxury goods or services,
- an unwritten rule to refrain from ostentation.

Their influence on Dutch behaviour is dealt with in Chapter 5 "A No-no: Privileges and Status Symbols ".

The "Cultural Revolution" of the 1960's and 1970's

The expression "cultural revolution" is linked to the great upheaval in Mao-Tse-Tung's China in 1966. At the same time, however, the winds of change also blew across Europe. A new generation, which had not been marked by the Second World War, started to revolt against the "Establishment". On May 13th, 1968, one million students and workers marched trough the streets of Paris shouting "Ten years is enough!".

In Holland, the middle of the 1960's marked the end of the post-war reconstruction period and the beginning of a cultural and social revolution. It started with students condemning the hierarchical structure of the universities. The year following the French riots, 600 angry Amsterdam students occupied the buildings of the university. Supported by politicians of the left, protest movements surged everywhere in the 70's, some of them bearing an anarchist signature. Young artists disturbed the elegant concerts of the famous ConcertgebouwOrchestra; squatters occupied empty houses and buildings; soldiers organised themselves into trade unions.

The Dutch monarchy came under fire. Riots erupted in Amsterdam during the wedding ceremonies of Princes Beatrix, and again in 1980 when she was crowned Queen of the Netherlands.

Political parties with a socialist bent flourished, and, in 1973, a socialist, Drs Joop den Uyl, became Prime Minister. He proclaimed the aims of his government as follows:
"We shall strive to spread, (i.e. re-distribute) income, property, knowledge, power and authority."

To underline the new, egalitarian policy, the government decreed that the forthcoming salary increases for employees would be a fixed amount for everybody (fl. 30,- per month), irrespective of salary level.

It also became a must for every left-wing intellectual to be strongly anti-American and to praise the Soviet-Union, Castro, Che Guevara and the "enlightened" social system of East Germany.

Later governments found it difficult to control the forces of dissent which had been unleashed. In 1980, it took a fierce police force of a thousand men, supported by armoured cars, tanks and bulldozers, to evict squatters from a building in Amsterdam.

From the mid-eighties onwards, however, the momentum of the "cultural revolution" petered out. A new generation of youngsters opted for studying, working and making a career instead of demonstrating. When the Berlin Wall fell in 1989, the credibility of the socialist parties became increasingly eroded. Government saw the need for the Dutch economy to become more productive in order to meet the threats of open borders and globalization. The businessman and industrial manager who were previously vilified as "dirty capitalists exploiting the working force" were rehabilitated.

Even the royal family gained supporters. A recent opinion poll showed that more than 90% of Dutch citizens are in favour of the monarchy!

Today (1996), the cultural and social revolution of the sixties belongs to the past, but a number of *"egalitarian ideals and practices"* can still be found in Dutch society and business life.

CHAPTER 3

Rank and Hierarchy Ignored

There is a Dutch expression for people who display a strong adherence to certain forms of behaviour:
"Dat is hem met de paplepel ingegeven" (he was given that in his baby-food).

One collective form of behaviour which they all tend to display, and which is taught them in their cradles, is a suspicion of rank and hierarchy.

Childhood upbringing

In distant places, British and Dutch expatriates of the Shell oil company live in special residential quarters, where each national group has its own primary school for employees' children. At the end of the school day, when the British children are leaving the building, you hear them saying *"Goodbye, Miss Smith,"* to their teacher in polite tones. At the other door, the Dutch children are shouting *"Bye-bye, Johanna!"*

In Holland, it is indeed quite common that children and students call their teacher by his or her first name. Even at home, there are families where the youngsters

"I always tried to bring my children up as
sturdy, self-sufficient, independent people."
"And did it work?"

"Yes, I never see them anymore."

Sigmund / Peter de Wit

do not address their parents as *"Mom"* or *"Dad"* but
call them by their first name. In her doctorate thesis on
"Parenthood in the 1990's", the Dutch educationalist
J. Doornenbal writes that parents attach more import-
ance to their child being "spontaneous and open" than

"obedient". They worry more about their offspring "communicating easily with other children" and "confiding in me when they have a problem" than "do they show respect for others?" or "do they behave correctly?".

W. Luyendijck, "NRC Handelsblad", 15 February 1996.

Expatriates in Holland, whose own culture places great value on children being obedient, deferential and disciplined, may be shocked by the lack of respect shown by Dutch youngsters. However, this freedom within education stimulates personal initiative. Enterprising Dutch youngsters and students can be found sipping tea with monks in Kathmandu, Nepal, or crossing the Sahara desert in an old Jeep.

In the social environment

The egalitarian Dutch are not very well suited to jobs which require serving other people, like waiters, receptionists and taxi-drivers. Although friendly by nature, they sometimes feel the need to make it perfectly clear that they are fully equal to the patrons they are serving. They also have an aversion for strict hierarchical structures.

Many Dutch catholics disapprove of the authoritarian way the Vatican appoints bishops without much regard for the wishes of the local catholic organisations. They do not dispute the right of the Pope to

nominate the bishops, but feel they should participate
in the selection procedure.

This even applies to the army:

> In 1995, it was decided to set up a combined Ger-
> man-Dutch army corps within the framework of
> Nato. After having exercised together for a number
> of months, both sides were asked by staff-members
> of Central Headquarters how they felt about work-
> ing together with the other nationality.
>
> *The Germans* were surprised by the lack of polite-
> ness shown by the Dutch soldiers, by their insuffi-
> cient respect for rank and position, by their sloppy
> way of dressing. Also mentioned were "too much
> discussion and to little action".
>
> *The Dutch* were sometimes irritated by the fact that
> under no circumstances would the Germans deviate
> from established rules; by their lack of interest in im-
> provisation, and their penchant for hierarchy and
> clear orders.
>
> *"NRC Handelsblad"*, *August 15th, 1995.*

But here, also, the "hippie" trend is being reversed. In
August 1996, the commanding officer of the Dutch Air
Force decreed that, from then, members of the air
force were prohibited from having long hair or wear-
ing ear-rings.

It should be mentioned, though, that in NATO ma-
noeuvres Dutch units perform to full satisfaction, so

looser discipline may be compensated for by good team-work and personal initiative.

In the business environment

There is no such thing as a homogeneous "business culture". The playing-field comprises large and small actors, conservative and innovative firms, local and multinational corporations, and, of course, the public service. There is, therefore, a great deal of variation in the culture of business. Applicants for a job with an advertising agency would be wise to wear a "creative-looking" outfit to the interview, while those applying for a position with a bank have little chance of success if they show up without a jacket and tie.

The location of the firm, i.e. in the North, South or the West of the Netherlands, also has its influence.

INFORMALITY

In most Dutch offices, however, there is little formality. Colleagues address each other with the informal "you" ("je"), and first names are used. When calling a travel agency, hotel or car rental company the person answering the phone will say: "Airport Hotel, you are speaking to Hans (or Sonia or Christine)". This informality is not restricted to colleagues or clients, but in many offices the boss, and even the boss' boss, is called by his first name.

When the former German ambassador was interviewed on a t.v. talk show, the first remark of the show-master was: "you don't mind if I call you (by your first name) Otto, do you?

A General Manager who came to Holland from the Far East was flabbergasted when one of his assistants entered his office one morning without bothering to knock and sat on the corner of his desk to show him a new product.

This might not happen everywhere, but, in many firms, it is considered normal that the boss should leave the door of his office ajar, to show that he is not

cutting himself off from his staff. If there is a meeting or visit from an outside party, however, nobody will object to the boss having his door closed.

Secretaries are also less docile than in other countries. An expatriate from India who had been transferred by his multinational company to Holland, told a friend the following story:

> In order to increase the efficiency of his office, he asked his secretary to procure an answering machine. She just flatly refused! (Perhaps he did not realise that she might have felt threatened by the use of a device which would have taken away part of her work).

In general, employees are more outspoken than in Latin or Asian countries. If they feel that the boss is wrong, they will not hesitate to tell him so. It may be that the social system, which makes it very difficult to dismiss anybody, also contributes to the lack of restraint when talking to superiors.

MANAGEMENT STRUCTURE: C.E.O. VS. "BESTUURSVOORZITTER"

The Dutch aversion to concentrating too much power in the hands of one individual is reflected in the way management is structured. There is a strong preference for collective management.

In the USA we know the figure of the "President and Chief Executive Officer", in France the "Président-Directeur Général, P.D.G.", and in the United Kingdom the "Managing Director". In Holland, most corporations have a "Board of Management" or a "Management Committee" where decisions are taken collectively. They are headed by a chairman who carries the title "Chairman of the Board of Management", in Dutch "Voorzitter van de Raad van Bestuur" or in newspaper jargon "Bestuursvoorzitter".

(An exception is the Philips Company where the Chairman of the Board of Management also carries the title of President).

> After a collective system of management had been introduced at the recently merged Anglo-Dutch publishing house "Reed-Elsevier", the British chairman resigned because, apparently, he could not get used to this new system.

Lately, as a result of the highly competitive climate due to the globalisation of business, even in Holland there began to be felt an increasing need for more visible leadership. The Chairman of the Board of Management is being increasingly compelled to leave the anonymity of the board-room and assume the role of inspired leader who rallies his troops around him.

THE MANAGEMENT TEAM

Another form of collective leadership is found in medium-sized and smaller companies, and in departments of larger firms. Here, the General Manager works closely with the other managers and heads of department in a so-called "Management Team", (though he has the last word in all decisions). This Team meets weekly or fortnightly to discuss all pending matters and future plans and its decisions are often published as "decisions of the Management Team".

A corporation which owns various large plants in Holland, will, as a rule, have an M.T. in each plant consisting of the Plant Manager, the Production Manager, the Human Resources Manager and perhaps also the Chief Engineer. In some cases, this M.T. will participate in decision-making, in others it will function as an advisory body to the Plant Manager. Thus, when a position for a manager is advertised, the list of requirements usually contains the item:

> "must be able to act as a good colleague within the Management Team".

For an expatriate General Manager, it may require some patience to adapt to this team concept. There is, however, an advantage. Once his decisions are supported by the Management Team, they will find a more ready general acceptance.

UNIVERSITY DEGREES

Knowing the egalitarian attitude of the Dutch, it is not surprising that Directors and Government Ministers are not addressed as "Herr Direktor" or "Monsieur le Ministre". There is, however, a group of individuals who like to differentiate themselves from the others, viz. those who have attended University and obtained a degree. This degree is mentioned everywhere: on all official publications, visiting cards, membership lists and obituaries. It should also be including when addressing formal letters, and even in more traditional companies, on internal memos and notes. Thus, if you send a message to your financial controller (who has studied economics) with a copy to your plant manager (who has a Master of Science degree) you should address it to:

| | Drs J. Janssen |
| copy | ir A. Smit |

As some firms have decided to dispense with this custom, it is prudent, as a newcomer, to enquire which form is appropriate.

It should be noted that these titles are not used in verbal communication, except for "Dokter" when you talk to your physician, and "Professor" when you address a University Professor. Policemen are usually addressed as "Agent".

Dutch university degrees

| Title | | Corresponding degree in |
Abbrev.	In full	Anglo-Saxon countries
drs	doctorandus	Masters Degree
mr	meester	Masters Degree in law
ir	ingenieur	Master of Science, graduated from a Dutch University of Technology
dr	doctor	Ph.D., LL.D., etc.

Other degrees

| Title | | Corresponding degree in |
Abbrev.	In full	Anglo-Saxon countries
ing.	ingenieur	Bachelor of Science, graduated from an Institute of Technology
RA	register accountant	Chartered accountant

Notes
1. The above abbrevations are placed *in front of* the name except R.A. which is placed *after* the name.
2. The abbreviations are not followed by a full stop, except "ing."

NOBILITY

Surprisingly enough, titles and ranks of nobility are still officially listed within anti-authoritarian Dutch society. The law of the Netherlands recognises the existing titles of peerage and regulates the rights to the title and to the succession. The last amendment voted by parliament in 1993, states that the title has to be mentioned on all official documents unless the owner has expressly requested otherwise.

"De Telegraaf", 20 October, 1993

Ambtenaren in Kampen echte koffieleuten

Civil servants in Kampen understand "The Coffee Break."

WILT U VANMIDDAG TERUGBELLEN? WIJ HEBBEN NU KOFFIEPAUZE.

BERTWITTE

"Sorry sir, could you call back this afternoon? We're on our coffee-break."

Current titles of nobility are (in order of ascending rank):
- Jonkheer
- Ridder
- Baron
- Graaf
- Prins

The title "Prins" is reserved for members of the Royal Family. For "Jonkheer", the abbreviation Jhr. is often used. Other titles are always written in full. As with university degrees, the title is not used during verbal communication.

There are still quite a number of rules of etiquette on how to address learned and noble members of society, either in writing or verbally, but they are slowly falling into disuse, except in diplomatic circles.

CHAPTER 4

Everybody Wishes to Be Consulted

"The right to be heard"

On the agenda of any Dutch meeting, the last item is invariably the "Rondvraag". Having dealt with all matters on the agenda, the Chairman offers every participant an additional opportunity to speak up on any matter he has on his mind.

To be asked for one's opinion and to be allowed to give advice is considered a basic right by every true-minded Dutchman. A special word is currently being used for it, viz. "inspraak", meaning "to participate in the decision-making process by giving one's view". It differs from the English "consensus", applied in Japanese business culture, because it does not stipulate that the final decision taken has to be accepted by everybody.

The "right to be heard" is also found in the parent-child relationship. When children have reached their teens, the giving of orders by their parents, such as "go and wash the dishes, and don't argue!" is replaced by discussion and negotiation.

The Dutch writer Nicolaas Matsier notes in a newspaper article that the use of the imperative mode has all but disappeared in Holland: "the only domain where the imperative can still be used are the military barracks and the cookery-book. (Although I even have doubts about the barracks.)"
"NRC Handelsblad", February 1996

"Inspraak" in the social and political environment

The government's decision to carry out large infra-structural projects is often delayed for months or years by the required procedure for "inspraak". All people, communities and municipalities affected by the project must be given the opportunity to comment on it, which usually results in a multitude of protests and proposals for amendment. When, for instance, the Government decided to build a new railway track from Rotterdam to the German border to cope with the expected growth of railway cargo to and from the "Ruhrgebiet", it took almost 5 years to agree:
– whether the new track was at all necessary
– on the exact route of the new line.

A study showed that if all "inspraak"-procedures are used to the maximum, the total delay may come up to 20 years.

Another form of "inspraak" is the referendum.

All major government parties had agreed that re-
grouping the municipality of Amsterdam and its surrounding villages into a larger unit would make the
administration of the urban unit more effective.
The proposal was, however, put to the citizens concerned through a referendum. When the outcome
showed more "nays" than "ayes", the Government
had to shelve the plan.

Appointments without any form of consultation are
also frowned upon:

In the Netherlands, the mayor of any city, town, or
other municipality is not elected by its inhabitants,
but appointed by the Government. The member of
the Cabinet responsible for the selection is the Minister of the Interior (Home Secretary).

To soften the impact of this "authoritarian" system,
the following "inspraak"-procedure is followed:

1. The municipal council makes a list of qualities
and qualifications which the new mayor should
possess, including age, experience, political views etc.
This "profile" is then sent to the Governor of the
province in which the town is located.

2. After taking note of the wishes of the council, the
Governor selects a number candidates.

3. The municipal council then appoints a committee, made up of a few of its members, who interview
the candidates proposed by the Governor.

Their findings are reflected in a survey which classifies the candidates into three groups:
- very suitable
- suitable
- unsuitable

and which is sent back to the Governor.

4. The Governor then selects three candidates, whose names, ranked in order of preference, are forwarded to the Minister of the Interior.

5. The Minister makes the final choice and informs the Governor, the municipal council and, of course, the successful candidate.

Of course, the Minister is supposed to take into account the wishes of the municipal council and if he does not—for political reasons—he may expect a wave of protests.

"Inspraak" in the Business Environment

MEETINGS GALORE

To most expatriates, the quantity of time spent in and on meetings is one of the most striking features of Dutch business life. They feel that a lot of valuable time is needlessly spent sitting—with the indispensable cup of coffee—and letting everybody give his views over and over again, often without reaching a clear and unequivocal decision.

The Dutch Research Institute for Recreation and Tourism has calculated that, every year, 13 million people (the total population of the Netherlands is 15 million) participate in 430,000 external meetings in hotels, restaurants and conference centres. For the organisers of such gatherings, there is a 363 page guide showing the location of thousands of suitable places. The total estimated cost of these meetings, 8.5 billion guilders a year, is only the tip of the iceberg. Experts estimate that the cost of in-house meetings is a multiple of this amount.

> The ABN AMRO bank maintains 36 meeting-rooms which can accommodate 25 people, and one reception hall for 400 guests at its Amsterdam head-office. This allows a total of 1,300 people to gather at the same time.
> *Annemarie van Hooft & Eric Vrijsen in "Elsevier",*
> *10 April 1993.*

Besides occupying a significant part of the working day, this also means that external contacts are hampered. To start the week with a meeting to discuss the activities planned for that week is a ritual in most companies. Thus, reaching a businessman by telephone on a Monday morning can be a trying experience. He will be either in a "Meeting of the Management Team" or "a Meeting of the department head with his surbordi-nates".

THE MEETING CULTURE HAS A LONG HISTORY

In the 15th and 16th century, Dutch provinces and a few large towns had already obtained a great deal of autonomy. Their governing bodies dealt with financial matters, such as the setting and collecting of taxes, trade affairs, and foreign policy, as well as helping to recruit soldiers for their sovereign. Thus, the king or emperor had to negotiate with them on a large number of issues.

Successive rulers of the Low Countries, from the Dukes of Burgundy to the Emperor Charles V, tried to revoke much of this autonomy by taking measures to strengthen their grip on the provinces and towns. But this only led to revolt. In the second half of the 16th century, the Northern part of the region—the "Netherlands" of to-day—broke off its allegiance to the Spanish sovereign. After that, in the absence of a central authority within the newly formed Dutch Republic, the provinces and large towns were compelled to switch over to total self-governance. As parliamentary democracy did not yet exist, the various power groups, such as the local aristocracy, the church, the guilds, the military establishment etc., had to get together and devise an effective system of administration. This entailed a large number of institutionalised meetings, where representatives of all groups could give their views and where decisions were taken mainly through negotiation.

This process of organised meetings is described in the book *"Nederland als Vergaderland"* by *Wilbert Van Vree.*

An important point made by Van Vree is that the Dutch "vergadering" is not exactly the equivalent of the English "meeting". The word "meeting" covers a wide field of collective gatherings whereas "vergadering" is limited to the assembly of people who have come together to agree upon future actions and policies.

THE REFORMATION ALSO LED TO MORE MEETINGS

The Reformation also had a strong influence on the culture of "vergaderen". In contrast to the Catholic church, which has a strictly hierarchic structure, the Protestants organised themselves on the basis of an elected collective leadership at all levels.

Needless to say, this system called for a plethora of regular meetings, for which detailed rules were laid down. In the regulations of the Church council of the town of Dordrecht, published in 1573, for example, the following rules about discipline can be found:

- anybody arriving late will be fined
- members taking the floor without permission by the chair will equally be fined
- even the chairman is liable to be fined if he omits to write down the conclusions of the meeting.
  From *"Nederland als Vergaderland"*, page 104.

CONSULTATION THROUGH MEETINGS HAS ITS ADVANTAGES

The Dutch tendency to reach decisions by way of consultation and negotiation, rather than by open confrontation where the strongest party prevails, also has positive points. If employees are given the opportunity to express their points-of-view, they will—reluctantly— accept a final decision, even if it differs from what they had proposed. Moreover, better communication between the manager and his employees allows him to know what is going on in his department and helps create group loyalty.

Indeed, the Dutch system is becoming one of the new patterns of modern management:

> In his book *"Reengineering Management"*, the American management consultant *James Champy* expresses the need for modern management to inform and motivate people on all levels and increase their participation in the decision making process.

Hierarchal structures with strictly regulated decision making are not working any more.

For a foreign manager, to scrap most meetings because "they are a waste of time" would not be advisable, though there is certainly enough scope in practically every Dutch company for streamlining existing habits.

To mention a few possible measures:
- reducing the frequency of fixed meetings
- circulating the agenda well in advance (possibly with attached position papers)
- reducing the number of items on the agenda by leaving out those points which do not constitute significant issues
- requesting one of the participants (prior to the meeting) to open the discussion by listing the pros and cons of the point at issue
- to limit the discussions on a "hot" subject by referring it to a small working-group, etc.

There is, however, one type of meeting which cannot be streamlined, viz. the meeting with the "ondernemingsraad".

THE "ONDERNEMINGSRAAD"—THE WORKS COUNCIL

In trade and industry, the informal consultation culture is complemented by a formal "inspraak" proce-

dure laid down in the Law on the works councils, the
"Wet op de ondernemingsraden", enacted in 1973.
Every firm with more than 50 employees must have an
"ondernemingsraad" (O.R.). This is the official organ
for consultation (and in some cases co-determination)
between management and employees, whose import-
ance is obvious from the fact that, at official events and
celebrations, its chairman is sometimes invited to sit
side-by-side with the management.

Although the main elements of the employees' con-
tracts of employment—such as salary levels and working hours—are negotiated with the trade unions, the
law stipulates that management has to provide the "ondernemingsraad" with a great deal of information, and
must request its advice—in certain cases, and even its
approval—on some proposed actions and measures.

Information
Twice a year management must supply the O.R. with
information on the firms' financial results, its expecta-
tions for the forthcoming period, a report on personnel and social activities, and forecasts for the years to
come, including the expected size of the work force.
For reasons of confidentiality, members of the O.R.
can be instructed to keep this information secret for a
certain period of time.

Advice

Before any decision is taken management has to ask for the advice of the o.r. in all matters relating to:
- major reorganisations
- changes in management
- major expansions, mergers, or other changes in the activities of the firm
- etc. etc.

The list includes the dismissal and appointment of top executives. Thus, the expatriate sent to Holland as

The Plant Manager at Philips Sittard and the chairman of the Works Council open the photo exhibition "50 years Philips Sittard".

General Manager of a Dutch company will have to wait for the advice of the o.r. before he can officially take over.

Should the o.r. hand in a negative advice, then the appointment can still be effected, but it will mean a more difficult start for the new manager.

As a matter of fact, management can overrule any negative advice handed in by the o.r. However, in a number of specific cases, the latter has the possibility to lodge an appeal with a Dutch court.

Approval
The approval of the o.r. is required prior to implementing any changes in existing regulations relating to:
– vacations
– safety and well-being
– profit-sharing schemes for the employees
– job evaluation systems
– etc. etc.

From the above description of the activities and the rights of the o.r., it will be clear that the General Manager will have to dedicate more than just a few days a year to this aspect of labour relations. But along with the undeniable delays in decision-making that result, there are also advantages:
– decisions taken after the o.r.'s approval can be
  smoothly implemented

– the O.R. may put forward positive suggestions on
   better organisation of the working environment.

In view of the intricacy of the matter and of possible
language problems, the expatriate General Manager
will usually delegate dealings with the O.R. to his
H.R.M. officer or personnel manager. He should re-
alise, however, that in case of serious problems, the
O.R. will insist on his personal intervention. In those
circumstances, it might help if the General Manager
has previously established good personal contacts with
the members of the O.R.

CHAPTER 5

A No-no: Privileges and Status Symbols

No privileges for the "high and the mighty"

"The cabinet minister in charge of police affairs, Hans Dijkstal, was probably sleeping in the back of his car whilst his driver raced on the highway at a speed of 160 km (100 m.p.h.). Both ministers (he was accompanied by the Minister of Justice) were caught by journalists driving 160 km per hour between The Hague and Rotterdam on Highway A12, where a speed limit of 120 km is in force."
"De Telegraaf", April 3rd, 1996.

In Holland, journalists always keep a close watch on all dignitaries so that even the smallest privilege is immediately brought to the public attention and condemned. Thus the Chairman of the Lower House of Parliament was reprimanded because he had ordered for himself and his visitors "de luxe cookies" costing fl.0.50 apiece, whereas other members of the House only got pre-packed cookies with their coffee!
"De Telegraaf", February 8th, 1996.

In the business environment

The same disapproval of privileges is found in business life, an exception being those prerogatives which can be considered necessary for carrying out the job.

PARKING PLACES

In neighbouring Germany, it would be unthinkable that "Herr Direktor" does not have a reserved parking-place for his car. The opposite is true in egalitarian Holland.

Many medium-sized and smaller companies do not allocate parking places at all, and everybody—including management—has to find a place for him or herself.

However, there are variations to this convention:
- A large Dutch bank allocates a restricted number of parking places to each department, and the employees of that department have to decide who may use them. In one case, the members gallantly decided to allocate the eight available parking spots to their eight female employees.
- Another formula used in a large corporation is to take into account, besides rank, a number of additional criteria, such as:
  - the number of years the employee has been working for the firm,
  - the distance from his home to the office,
  - whether he has to use his car often during working hours.

Thus, an assistant manager, having made his career within the firm, may have an allocated space, whereas a recently-appointed manager may not.

CANTEENS

In smaller companies, managers eat in the employees' canteen, like everybody else. At most, they will have a reserved table in a corner. In larger corporations, managers may avail themselves of a separate lunchroom, prudently called the "Guests' lunchroom".

Status symbols

The "we are all equal" attitude of the rowdy 1960's and 1970's is still present in many aspects of business life (and politics), but in a less dogmatic way. Pragmatism, as well as harsh economic reality, have tempered the voice of idealists and utopians, and differentiation is beginning to be accepted, or at least, tolerated. The time is past when the Minister or Managing Director came to the office on his bicycle. Still, flashy status symbols are taboo, and to-day's Cabinet Ministers are limited in their choice of government car put at their disposal: a Ford Scorpio is all right, a de-luxe Mercedes is out.

> When the Minister for Traffic and Transport declared that she thought a large Mercedes should be added to the list, she was strongly rebuked by public opinion. Everybody shouted "shame".

Status symbols in business

To a degree, status symbols are accepted in most companies, especially if a functional reason can be found. An assistant-manager promoted to manager will often get a larger office—or an office to himself if he was previously sharing his room with others—with the explanation that he now has to conduct more meetings and interviews which require space and privacy. But too much ostentation is frowned upon, and this applies in particular to the most visible and emotionally-linked status symbol: the company car.

COMPANY CARS

For salesmen and sales managers there are functional arguments for the choice of a car. If the representative has to carry samples, then a break type or station-wagon will be provided. For the others, an acceptable cost per km is laid down, and models and types will be chosen which do not exceed that cost. Though some companies, in order to attract the best available salesmen, offer a slightly more expensive car.

For the Managing Director there are less functional arguments to defend the choice of his car, so if he is driving a Cadillac, Bentley or large Mercedes, this will be considered excessive. A large Volvo or BMW "5" class is thought to be good enough.

Asked by a friend why he was driving a medium-sized car instead of a larger one, the Managing Director of a Dutch printing house replied: "In the 20 years I have been working in this company, I have built up a very good relationship with all of our 90 employees. They believe that this car is large enough for their boss and they would strongly disapprove if I were to buy a larger one."

Another example is the expatriate from an Austrian trading firm sent to Amsterdam to take charge of their local office. After he had chosen a Mercedes as company car, his employees went to see him and said: *"look here, we are a small company and a Mercedes is much too expensive a car for you!"*

Clever car distributors adapt their publicity to this situation. The Swedish firm, "Volvo", for instance, advertises their top model 960 with the following words:
"... in these modern times a too flashy car only irritates the members of your own organisation as well as your customers; therefore Volvo offers you a low-profile car with superb comfort and luxury."

An exception to the above are the President and top executives of large corporations. Their favourite car is the large BMW.

DRESS

In an American travel guide, the following advice could be found:
"The straightforward Dutch are suspicious of ostentation or people who care too much about their ap-

pearance. Dress is far less formal than in other parts
of Europe so be careful not to overdress."

In France, "le patron" is easily recognised by the fact
that he wears more expensive clothes and is shown respect by his subordinates. In Holland, it is much more
difficult, when entering an office, to find out who is
the manager by looking at dress or behaviour.

Blue jeans have lost some of their popularity and are
mostly worn nowadays by the young and by members
of the artistic professions. In the office, tie and jacket
prevail, but the latter is not always in view. It is generally taken off upon entering the office and neatly sus-
pended on a hanger, only to be put on upon departure
or when an important customer is announced.

The Technical University of Eindhoven publishes a
guide for foreigners coming to study or work in Eindhoven, called "Eindhoven Survival Kit".

On behaviour, habits and traditions, they state:
" The Dutch (...) seem to attach little value to style
and outward appearance. (...) Since the sixties, cloth-
ing and appearance have no longer been indicators
of someone's social status or background".

CHAPTER 6

Pragmatic and Direct

Pragmatic

When trying to understand the Dutch, expatriates are often baffled by the apparent contradictions they encounter. This is due to the fact that there are two prototypes of Dutchmen:
– the preacher and moralist
– the practical businessman.

In some aspects of life, the preacher can clearly be recognised, whereas, in others, it is the no-nonsense salesman who prevails.

Levying taxes is a good example of pragmatism. Income-tax in the Netherlands is amongst the highest of Europe, but the effects are somewhat softened by the rule that one may deduct from one's taxable income all costs which are deemed necessary to maintain that income. Thus, a scientist may deduct the cost of all publications and books he has to buy in order to keep up-to-date on new developments.

For many years, a known criminal made use of this facility and deducted from his declared income the cost of his gun and his pitbull terrier, which he said he needed for his protection. The deduction was fully accepted by the tax authorities. When questions arose in parliament about this dubious practice, the tax inspector pointed out that it was his duty to correctly apply the tax laws and not to pass any moral judgements! But even pragmatism has its limits, and when the story made the news, the public outcry forced the government to call a halt to this sort of practice.

Another example of the practical approach appeared on the front page of the newspaper "de Telegraaf". Under the heading "Tax on paid-for sex", it told its readers:

"Dutch sex clubs are working together with the income tax department to devise a satisfactory regulation for collecting tax on paid-for sex.

This new regulation should generate an additional income from taxes of approximately 250 million guilders. For the customers it will bring about an average price-increase of 15% ("!")

Points still to be discussed are the professional expenses prostitutes may deduct (from taxable income) such as dresses, make-up, medical expenses ...

"De Telegraaf" November 4th 1995. Translation D. Pappenheim.

Bureaucracy vs. practicality

Pragmatism, it would seem, is at odds with the Dutch penchant for establishing detailed rules and regulations for everything, leading to a vast quantity of bureaucracy.

At a meeting of industry leaders with members of the government, the former illustrated their complaint about excessive regulations in the building sector by having two wheelbarrows pushed into the conference-room, each stacked five feet high with books and brochures. These, they explained, were the laws and regulations which each builder has to know and observe!

But in many cases, the practical Dutch find a way to circumvent bureaucracy.

"It is a national habit to complain about the complicated rules from the ministry and to modify them to fit local circumstances when appropriate. There is a bit of larceny in the Dutch soul. Though it is widely recognised that compliance with the rules keeps the country afloat, in practice most people act as though slavish adherence isn't necessary, at least in their case. Amsterdam is the city where this tendency is most visible."

Loren S. Barritt, "An Elementary School in Holland".

Sometimes even the government recognises that laws may be difficult to obey. For theses cases, they have coined the word "gedogen". The dictionary translates this as "to tolerate, permit, suffer, allow", but in practice "gedogen" means: "we recognize that this law or rule is awkward, so the police and other government inspectors have been told to look the other way."

In the case of moral and religious issues where principles and dogmas are at stake, such as euthanasia, abortion and drugs, lawmakers tend to look for some sort of compromise which will not make one of the parties too unhappy. As this is practically impossible, it leads to complicated and unclear laws, where the judge is often called to be the final arbitrator. In the case of drugs, a practical compromise was found to satisfy both those citizens who are strongly against the use of any drug and those who advocate the liberalisation of soft drugs:

– Dealing and trading in any kind of drug is a criminal offence, but using soft drugs in small quantities is allowed. This gives rise to the question: "from where does the private person using soft drugs get supplied in a legal way?" The only logical answer seems to be that every user has to have a few cannabis-plants on his balcony! Though this policy is critised by other governments, the number of junkies in the Netherlands is low compared with that in a number of other European countries.

Straightforward and direct in business

Foreign businessmen often have to get used to the Dutch lack of subtlety and nuance. To be straightforward and direct, both in business and private life, is considered a virtue.

In Latin and Asian countries, it is customary to get acquainted before getting down to business. This may take a few hours or a few days. In France, business talks are invariably interrupted for an extended lunch, during which all topics of a general nature may be

raised except the business deal at hand. It is only when
the desert is served, "entre la poire et le fromage", that
the subject of business may prudently be reverted to.
To the average Dutch businessman, all this "rigma-
role" is a loss of time. Business talks must be to the
point, and "beating around the bush" should be
avoided. When welcoming a visitor from abroad, he
will ask.
1. How would you like your coffee?
2. Did you have a good trip?
and then start right away with the business at hand.

THE DIRECT APPROACH

Expatriates working in Holland should be prepared for
a very direct approach by their colleagues. Female expatriates from Latin countries are often shocked when,
on their first day at the office, they are asked: "how old
are you" and "are you married"? It often sounds like a
way of asking, "are you available?"

The indirect approach for ventilating criticism—so as
not to make the subject lose face—is seldom used.
Boss and colleagues will tell you what is on their mind
without mincing their words.

An American expatriate described it as follows:
Where we might tell an employee "I think you

might have done this differently", the Dutch will say "You were wrong".

Nevertheless, having got used to Dutch straightforwardness, many a foreign businessman starts to appreciate it.

"You do not lose time, business is briskly done and you know exactly where you stand".

DUTCH TIME

With the exception of the southern part of the Netherlands, mainly the province of Brabant, punctuality is required. Meetings start exactly on time and it is customary to arrive five to ten minutes early for an appointment. At certain lectures and conventions, coffee is served before the start of the meeting, so participants may arrive up to half-an-hour early. In Brabant, a delay of up to fifteen minutes is accepted, and is called the " Brabants' quarter of an hour". The same applies to University professors, who are known to start their lectures fifteen minutes after the time indicated.

Punctuality does not apply to most medical doctors and specialists, however. Even when an appointment has been made, waiting time ranges from 30 minutes to one hour, and it is prudent to take along reading matter and perhaps a sandwich.

Straightforward and direct in the social environment

"I remember that, on a certain evening (...) I was staying with a friend in the middle of the country. As it was late, he offered to drive me to Amsterdam, a distance of about 150 km. We covered that distance smoothly and comfortably, passing the time with small talk.

Just as we are going to enter the town, he deviated from the route he would normally take and, a few minutes later, stopped at the tramway station of line 25. 'There are trams from here,' he informed me very politely.

To drive the remaining 3 to 4 km, which still separated me from my home, would have seen to him as too obliging."   *Translation D. Pappenheim.*

Thus writes the Portuguese journalist *J. Rentes de Carvalho* in his book *"Waar die andere God woont"*, which describes the hardships he suffered when having to adapt to the Dutch way of life.

The gallantry and refinement found in the Latin and Asian countries are admired in Holland, but as exotic fruit not suitable for transplantation into Dutch soil. It would nevertheless be wrong to conclude that Holland is a rude country. Most foreigners find their hosts friendly and courteous, but admit that they have to get used to the "direct and no-nonsense approach".

CHAPTER 7

Etiquette

The increase in business and holiday travel, as well as world-wide media coverage, have contributed to a certain convergence of customs and practices in social life. Nevertheless, there is quite a difference between being invited to a French home "pour le dîner" or to a Dutch residence for a "drink and a snack".

Introducing yourself

At meetings, receptions and parties, the Dutch seldom wait to be introduced by a common friend. They take the initiative to approach the other party, shake hands and state their name. (In more formal circles, the family name only, otherwise first and last name.) Women also introduce themselves, and if seated, some will stand up. Because the rules with regard to who introduces himself first are not very strict, both parties often speak simultaneously and one, or both, do not get the names straight. In those cases, it is perfectly acceptable to ask that it be repeated. The word "aangenaam", corresponding to "pleased to meet you"—in French "enchanté(e)"—should be avoided.

The situation is different when you are invited for the first time to a private party or dinner. Assuming that you do not know any of the other guests, the hostess will introduce you to a few of the persons present in order to establish initial contact.

Being invited by Dutch friends

FOR A CUP OF COFFEE

"Do drop in for a cup of coffee" is a general invitation to informal social contact. In some regions and circles, it can be taken literally, but to be on the safe side, it is preferable to ask: "which day and time would be convenient?".

The coffee visit usually takes place in the morning, starting between 10.30 and 12 a.m. Together with the coffee, cake or cookies will be offered. Should the coffee invitation have a festive character (such as birthdays which are always celebrated), then pastries and pies will be served. Sometimes, after coffee, a glass of white wine is offered, together with a snack.

FOR LUNCH

As lunch in Holland is frugal, invitations for lunch are not frequent. One may, nevertheless, be asked to come (around midday) for "a cup of coffee and a sandwich" in which case, a sandwich, as well as a cup of soup or a warm snack will generally be served. In the less frugal South, such a lunch is called "Brabantse koffietafel" and will offer a greater variety of sandwiches and warm snacks, including fruit and—in special cases—a glass of Dutch geneva or white wine.

FOR AFTERNOON TEA

Tea as a social event, with freshly buttered scones and cucumber sandwiches, is not part of Dutch tradition. Afternoon tea, starting at 4 p.m., means tea with pastries or a slice of cake, and is less formal than in Anglo-Saxon countries. Quite often, once the cake has been eaten and the teapot emptied, drinks will be served, accompanied by mixed nuts and cheese crackers or a warm snack.

Time of departure: between 6.00 and 6.30 p.m.

FOR AN INFORMAL DINNER

The younger generation may invite each other "to our place after office hours for a drink and something to eat". The guest may offer to bring along a bottle of wine to this informal event. Drinks will start at 5.30 p.m. and homely food will be served around 6.30. As lunch is always a simple affair, the main meal in Holland is generally taken as early as 6 p.m or, at the latest 7.

FOR A FORMAL DINNER

The more formal dinner invitation is not so common any more, as it requires a very special effort by the hostess (maids and charwomen being an almost extinct race). If invited to dinner, the following aspects should therefore be noted.

Time

Your host will tell you what time you are expected, usually around 7 p.m. If you are used to the Latin way of arriving at least half an hour late, you should be aware that in Holland one is expected to be punctual. The only exception is the town of the Hague where the unwritten rule says you should arrive five minutes late. This punctuality is important for foreign hostesses, who have invited their Dutch friends, especially because the latter may even ring the bell ten minutes ahead of time! Being ready a quarter of an hour in advance is always a good idea.

Flowers

If invited for the first time, flowers are best brought along. Contrary to Germany and Sweden, where the protective wrapping has to be removed before handing

the bouquet to the hostess, in Holland the wrapping, in most cases a transparent foil, should be left on.

Once one gets to know each other better, small gifts may be brought instead of flowers, such as a plant for the garden, a bottle of wine or a box of chocolates. Chocolates are, of course, appreciated, but one should take into account that quite a number of hostesses (and hosts) are on a slimming diet nowadays.

At dinner
Conversation is not unduly restricted, but topics such as money, religion and politics should be avoided unless they are broached by the host or hostess.

In Catholic families, a moment's silence used to be observed before starting to eat, allowing for a silent prayer. This habit is still found in a few traditional circles, mostly in the Southern provinces of Brabant and Limburg. In the North, some traditional Protestant families observe a moment's silence both at the beginning and at the end of the meal.

Wine
Before starting to drink, guests should wait for the host to raise his glass and bring out the first toast. If he is busy talking and forgets, his wife will signal him to do his duty. Thereafter, guests drink freely. If, in the course of the dinner, a different type of wine is being served—for example a red wine to follow a white one—the host should again raise his glass to signal that drinking can be resumed.

Thanking the hosts
In Scandinavian countries, guests must thank the hostess for the excellent meal before leaving the table. This is not the case in Holland, although it is perfectly acceptable to tell the lady of the house how nice the din-

ner has been when moving to the next room for coffee and liquors.

On leaving you should express your appreciation for the "gezellige" evening. It is also customary to phone the next day to tell the hostess how much you enjoyed the company, the food etc.

FOR A DRINK "EEN BORREL"

"Borrel" is, strictly, speaking the designation for Dutch gin (geneva), but it is also used as a generic name for "drinks". "Borrel"-time corresponds to the French "apéritif" and covers the period between 5 and 7 p.m. Together with the drinks, plates with nuts and cheese crackers will have been placed on the table; quite often small snacks will also be served. Guests should leave between 6.45 and 7 p.m. It may be that the host(ess) has prepared some warm snacks or a cup of soup, in which case the departure is delayed by half-an-hour or so.

If the invitation is for more than a drink, then it will be called "een borrel en een hap" (a drink and a bite). This is an affair which will start at 6 p.m. and may last until 10, or even later. The "bite" can be a cheese-and-salad buffet, or a salad and meat buffet, with a warm dish added. This may vary from a cup of soup or a piece of pizza to a plate of goulash and rice.

FOR A PARTY ("EEN FEEST")

A party is usually given to celebrate an event such as a birthday, wedding anniversary, house-warming party or any other festive occasion. It will last well through the evening and sometimes to the early hours of the morning. There are no strict rules to be followed, so a "feest" may range:

- from a students' party where bottles of booze and an assortment of cheese and bread are displayed for guests to help themselves, and an amateur disc-jockey creates the musical background,
- to a formal wedding anniversary, catered by a profes-sional firm, with a pianist playing soft cocktail music in the background.

The wording and quality of the invitation card will in-dicate what sort of party can be expected.

What to wear

There are few strict dress rules. Like everywhere else, young people will dress more informally, but even then, the great variety of dress at any social event is most fascinating to observe. If the invitation to a bar-becue or a Sunday coffee says "dress informal", then the choice of clothes is ample, excluding only a tie or Bermuda shorts.

Should your boss, friend or colleague ask you to a

"borrel", then a jacket with or without tie should be adequate. Most Dutchmen feel safe in a dark-blue blazer, which can be worn with a tie (formal) or with a cravat (less formal). Women should wear a dress, suit or deux-pièces to receptions and dinners. For the rest, follow the advice of an eminent Frenchman: "wear the dress you feel pretty in".

Presents

In some Latin-American and Asian countries, presents are received with a smile of gratitude or a bow, and opened only after the guests have left. In Holland, presents are always opened on the spot and thanked for warmly. The other guests will not hide their curiosity, and the recipient will proudly show the gift around.

An exception is found at wedding-receptions where, as a rule, presents are sent to the home of the bride prior to the wedding. If a guest brings a present to the reception, then it will be taken upon arrival by one of the members of the family, and placed, unopened, on a special table. This also applies to other types of receptions, jubilees, anniversaries etc. where presents might be taken along.

CHAPTER 8

"He Who Does Not Treasure the Dime Is Not Worthy of the Dollar"

"One coke with ten straws" is the title of a Belgian book about the Dutch. Some consider it a shortcoming, others a virtue, but all agree that the Dutch are tight-fisted. Their reputation is reflected in the well-known expressions "Going Dutch" and "Dutch treat".

Part of this attitude can be traced back to Calvinist doctrine, which called for a frugal lifestyle. A Dutch proverb says: "he who does not treasure the dime is not worthy of the dollar".

Do not, therefore, be surprised if you see a well-to-do matron giving her neighbour a lift to town, whereupon the neighbour proposes to share the cost of the gasoline. Or going shopping with your Dutch girl-friend in her car and spending twenty minutes or so looking for a parking place where there is no parking meter.

If invited to a traditional Dutch family for a cup of coffee, you will be allowed to take one cookie from the cookie-jar. Only when you are offered a second cup will a second cookie be offered.

THE TIGHT-FISTED QUEEN

In the days when royalty was synonymous with lavishness and luxury, many a Dutch monarch was careful about spending money. Queen Emma, for example, wife of William the Third, though German by birth, had been raised in the Calvinist tradition.

When arranging for the royal railway carriage to be coupled to the train for a journey to another part of the Netherlands, the stationmaster explained that the (usual) charge would be an amount corresponding to the price of ten first-class tickets. The Queen looked at him sternly.

"My good man," she said, "there will be only three of us travelling inside the carriage, so we shall pay you no more than the price of three tickets".

FRUGALITY DOES NOT EXTEND TO THE HOME

In Holland, the lady of the house takes pride in the carefully-arranged interior of the home, the expensive oak furniture, the indirect lighting, the large-screen television, the fireplace and the cupboard with souvenirs and other paraphernalia. Her husband, on the other hand, will explain that he installed and painted the false ceiling himself, as well as the large bookcase next to the door. Every self-respecting Dutchman considers himself a born handyman, and the few clumsy ones will never dare to admit that they do not own a toolset.

About half of Dutch families own their own home, since the government has been actively supporting the ownership concept by special tax facilities. This is, of course, an extra stimulant for making improvements that increase both the comfort and resale value of the residence. So it appears that the money saved by being parsimonious in public is spent instead inside the walls of the home.

Generous to the underdog

When it comes to aid for the poor, the unfortunate and the handicapped, however, Dutch purse-strings are easily loosened. There are a great many special schools for the mentally disadvantaged all over the country, and the government provides a large number of facilities, as well as financial aid, for the physically handicapped. Social security and welfare services see to it that everybody is assured of medical care and that a minimum living allowance is available to all.

The public is also large hearted and eager to help:
A young boy who was partly paralysed sent a letter to a television channel saying that he was a great fan of motorcycles and that his dearest wish was to be of-

fered a ride on one. Within three weeks, the T.V.
channel had called on the National Association of
Motorcycle Owners, and, on a Sunday morning,
500 motorbikes assembled in front of the boy's
home and gave him an unforgettable ride through
the countryside.

Various sports-clubs also teach mentally-disadvantaged
children and adults horse-riding and rowing. For elderly people who are not physically able to leave their
home, the Dutch Red Cross organises special boat
trips on rivers and lakes so they can enjoy the land-
scape.

COLLECTING MONEY "FOR A GOOD CAUSE"

"Our Under-secretary for Sport Affairs, Erica Terp-
stra, will kick-off the ball at the KsvK soccer cham-
pionship in Amsterdam-Noord. KsvK is the abbreviation of 'Children play for Children'.
For the whole day the junior players of a large number of clubs will play soccer in order to collect
money for their fellow children who are hospitalised
in the Amsterdam AMC Hospital."
"De Telegraaf", June 1st, 1996.

Not only sports clubs, but also schools motivate children to espouse a good cause and collect money for it.
More often than not this will be a project for building

a school in Tanzania, supporting a mission in Brazil, or sending X-ray equipment to a small hospital in the Philippines. To find children or students with a collecting-box at your front-door is an aspect of daily life; it is practical to have small change ready.

On a larger scale, it can happen that a television channel mobilises viewers in a 24 hour non-stop programme to donate money for a special purpose, such as famine relief in Africa. Companies, clubs and associations send their gifts to the T.V. station and by the end of the programme, the total amount may well be in excess of ten million guilders.

GOVERNMENT AID TO DEVELOPING NATIONS

There is national consensus that poor countries should also be helped. The Dutch Government earmarks an annual amount in excess of 0.8% of GNP for official Development Assistance. This percentage compares favourably with that of many a richer country, as can be seen from the following chart.

Official development assistance in % of GNP

	1990-1991
United States	0.20
France (including its overseas territories)	0.61
United Kingdom	0.30
Japan	0.32
Netherlands	**0.90**
Denmark	0.95
Sweden	0.91
Norway	1.15

From

Development Assistance Comittee, "Chairman's Report 1985-1992" as reproduced in the publication "*Normverva(n)ging*" of the Netherlands' Ministry of Foreign Affairs.

CHAPTER 9

What About Mrs. Expatriate?

For the business executive, to be posted abroad represents a challenge. Whether he has to set up a new company or expand the activities of an existing enterprise, he is expected to produce concrete results, such as improving profits, increasing market-shares or, preferably, a combination of both.

But for Mrs. Expatriate, the challenge is no less. She has to set up a household, take care of the children (schools, doctors, sports, birthday parties), build up a social life for herself, participate in the social life of her husband, and so forth. And all this in strange and sometimes incomprehensible surroundings!

If she speaks English, her problem may be less, but she will still find out that, although Holland ranks second in Europe where knowledge of foreign languages is concerned, 28% of the Dutch population does not speak any language besides their own.

From: "Eurobarometer No.28", December 1987, EEC.

There are two solutions to the problem:
- her children will have learned Dutch in a amazingly short time and can serve as interpreters (but, unfortunately, they are at school most of the day);
- She can learn enough Dutch to get along in daily life.

SCHOOLS

As mentioned in Chapter 4, school buses are practically unknown in Holland, since the basic attitude is that children should not be too protected from the realities of life, but should learn at an early age to cope with the harsh outside world.

The principal of a French boarding school used to address his pupils at the graduation ceremony as follows:

"You are now going to leave the safe harbour to sail into open waters ...".

This is not the way the Dutch see it.

During his study of the Dutch elementary school system, Professor Loren Barritt saw a boy at a Kindergarten playground fall, hit his head and begin crying. The Dutch teacher watched without taking any action, and later explained:

"We are not in control of all that goes on, particularly among the children. Life contains many diffi-

cult situations of dealing with others, particularly in
Holland where we all live cheek by jowl. The best
way to learn about them is to experience dealing
with them in school, and there is no better time to
begin than at the beginning".
From: "An Elementary School in Holland " by
L.S. Barritt.

In many countries, such as France, schools provide a
meal for every child at lunch time. This is not the case
in Holland: children carry sandwiches made by their
parents, as well as small change for a glass of lemonade,
coke or coffee. In most schools, a member of the staff
will stay on during the lunch break; in many smaller
ones, the parents will provide surveillance in turn.

NEIGHBOURS

In the United States, where moving from one place to
another is more frequent than in Holland, new settlers
are welcomed by their neighbours, who arrange
welcome-parties. In Holland, neighbours will seldom
take the initiative. They will wait for the newcomer to
make the first step. This may involve inviting the
neighbours for a cup of coffee a week or two after having arrived and settled down. Should the neighbour's
wife be at home during day-time, the newcomer might
ask her to drop in during the day, which is more casual. It might be, though, that her English is not fluent

and she might prefer to come accompanied by her husband.

THE METRIC SYSTEM

Switching over to the metric system will require an additional effort for those raised in the Commonwealth and the United States. Conversion tables are readily available but the exact figures, with 3 decimal places, are not always easy to memorise.

If we forget about the decimals, the following simplification may be useful.

Weight
– a Dutch pound ("pond") is somewhat heavier than the English pound (lb), viz. + 10%.
– 2 Dutch pounds make a Kilogram (kg), which is generally called "kilo". 1 Kilo therefore equals 2 English pounds + 10 %.
– Meat cuts, such as sliced ham, are mostly ordered by quantities of 100 grammes (gr). (A kg equals 1,000 gr)
– In most parts of the Netherlands they call 100 gr "één ons"; this has nothing to do with the English ounce (which equals 28 gr).

Volume
– A litre is slightly more than:
  – a quarter of a US gallon
  – a fifth of a UK gallon.

Length
– a metre (m) equals 3 feet + 10%
– a kilometre (km) equals about two-thirds of a mile.

Shopping, finally, is not much different in Holland, as supermarkets, department stores and discounters are very much alike all over the world.

CHAPTER 10

"Will the Real Dutchman
Please Stand Up ..."

In a book about Dutch culture, one might expect an answer to the question: what does the typical Dutchman look like?

"Les Hollandais sont grands, blonds et aiment les kermesses bruyantes" (The Dutch are tall, blond and they like noisy fairs),"
stated the authors of a French geography book used at the International School of Geneva in the 1950's.

But Paul Verlaine, the French poet, disagreed. After visiting the Netherlands in 1892, he published a booklet called "Quinze jours en Hollande," in which he stated:
"Enfin, voici un Hollandais comme on se le figure en France, et en Europe, je pense: Grand, gros, l'air réjoui, fumant une pipe énorme."
(Now there is a Dutchman as we imagine him in France, and in Europe I believe: tall, stout, looking happy and smoking an enormous pipe.)

But be he tall or stout, noisy or pipe-smoking, inside the hull are—as said before—not one, but two characters, who do not see eye-to eye and occasionally frown upon each others' actions and opinions. One is the preacher and the moralist, who is convinced that his rightful beliefs must be followed by everybody, and who will lecture friend and foe on how they should order their lives. He is unrelenting on issues such as non-discrimination, human rights and protection of the environment, and participates actively in Amnesty International, Greenpeace and the World Wildlife Fund.

The other one is the down-to-earth trader and no-nonsense businessman. In colonial times, the Spanish claimed South-America for their King and for the Catholic Church, and the English went to the East for the glory of their country. The Dutch, on the other hand, organised their expeditions to the East and West Indies purely as business ventures. Up to today, the enterprising Dutch businessman can be found putting up tents and temporary structures for the Olympic games in Atlanta, building greenhouses in Moscow, or dredging the harbour of Singapore.

It is not surprising that, to the foreigner, the Dutch character seems puzzling and full of contradictions.

In Amsterdam, the sex industry may be flourishing, but 60 km to the South, a home for the aged can be found where, on religious grounds, there are no radios or television sets.

But there is an aspect of Dutch culture which may help to solve the puzzle:

The Dutch are not fanatical

When facing each other in anger, they seldom take up the sword for a duel. Instead, they sit down, talk, and "sort it out together".

Bibliography

Barritt, Loren S. *"An Elementary School in Holland: Experiment in Educational Practice"*. (1996) Utrecht. International Books, Jan van Arkel.

Champy, James. *"Reengineering Management"*. (1995) New York. HarperCollins

Doornenbal, Jeanette. *"Ouderschap als onderneming"*. (1996) Jan van Arkel.

Hofstede, Geert, *"Cultures and Organizations, Software of the mind"*. (1991) Maidenhead, UK, McGraw-Hill.

Ramalho Ortigão. *"Holland 1883"* (1964) Utrecht/Antwerpen. Het Spectrum.

Rentes de Carvalho, J. *"Waar die andere God woont"*. (1972) Amsterdam. De Arbeiderspers.

Schama, Simon. *"The Embarassment of Riches"*. (1987) London. HarperCollins.

Technical University Eindhoven. *"Eindhoven survival kit"*. (1993) Eindhoven. Technische Universiteit.

Trompenaars, Fons. *"Zakendoen over de grens. Leren omgaan met andere culturen"* (1993) Amsterdam/Antwerpen. Contact.

Van Vree, Wilbert. *"Nederland als vergaderland: opkomst en verbreiding van een vergaderregime"*. (1994) Groningen. Wolters-Noordhoff.

Note Newspaper cuttings and exerpts from weekly magazines are listed within the text.